Be

Adrian Cox-Settles

Paperback ISBN: 978-0-578-37945-6

Published by Adrian Cox-Settles

Dedication

I want to dedicate this book to my Mommy.

Acknowledgements

First, I would like to thank Allah for his mercy, grace, and love.

Throughout my life I have been blessed with loving family members and friends who have been a source of encouragement, love, and support. I would like to acknowledge and thank:

- My husband Billy a great provider, always supporting me and cheering me on, always pushing our sons and me to our best.
- My three sons: Damion, Idris, and Jibril, whose unconditional love and support in all my endeavors helps to keep me motivated.
- My 3 children that I'd miscarried: Ihsan, Iman, and Noor. Mommy loves you and prays to see you all in heaven one day, Godwilling!
- My parents: My fighting spirit I got from my mother, Debra Ann Cox, a survivor in every sense of the word. I felt special when my father, Johnny Davis, Jr., made me feel like I was "Daddy's little girl". To my stepmother, Gloria Davis, for keeping me in the loop.
- My little brother, Johnny Cox, one of my fiercest protectors!
- My beloved grandmothers, Mama Bessie Cox, maternal grandmother, and Mrs. Emma Davis, paternal grandmother, my strong foundations. With loving care, they poured into me wisdom and strength.
- My Aunts Fern, Ivy, and Angie and cousins: Katrina, LaKesha, Tracy, Annee, Melvin, Teon, Colby, Jasmine, Rachel, and Shiloah who believed in me, appreciated me, and valued me. With their support I couldn't be discouraged.

- My Mom and Dad-in-laws Norma and Billy Settles Sr, and their families for their love and support.
- My Sister-in-law Tia for being available, supportive, understanding.
- My Sisters in Islam: Ayet, Najaah, and Terea. Sisters who became friends; friends who accepted me, with understanding and without judgement. Amongst my biggest cheerleaders. I love you all greatly.
- Zamiylah, Makkah, and Sumayah, for relating to me, caring for me, and being there when needed.
- Taheerah, Islaah and Ms. Mary for being supportive and giving.
- Shahira, for wanting the best for me unconditionally.
- Maysa, for seeing my value.
- Jahaira and Lynette, for appreciating me and keeping in touch.
- Tracye "Amira Saran" A. Howard: former colleague from the Baltimore City Public School System, sister, and friend who always has my back; great educational minds think alike, our collaborative genius works.
- My students past and present. It has been my honor and a privilege to work with you. The time I spent with you continues to inspire me to help students succeed in education in the traditional classroom and beyond.
- The Village: any other family and friends, associates, patrons, and anyone who has supported me through the years.

Table of Contents

Letter to My Bully

Dear Bully,
Why are you picking on me?
Is it that you see something that I don't see?
Is it that you want to be where I am?
Why me?
I never gave you a reason to focus on me.
I just want to be left alone!
To be myself and have fun.
To walk without looking over my shoulders.
I just want to be me and express myself freely.
Why do you want to keep me in your box?
I am not yours.
I am of something way greater than you.
You don't realize that I can only take but so much.
You are forcing me to react in a way that is not me.
You are forcing me to think of things that I've never thought of before.
You are forcing me to become someone else that I don't want to be.
You are pushing my back against the wall.
I can't stay in this position forever.
I must react.
I thought about all the things that I wanted to do to you.
I thought about all the things that I wanted to do to myself.
Sadly, those things felt good because I felt I could be in control.
I am tired of being reactive.
I want to be proactive.

I am not the helpless person that you think that I am.
I am your biggest threat because you got me to a point where I don't care.
I can take you and/or me out and it doesn't even matter.
The ball is in my court, and I must decide what to do with it.
I am running this show!
You are the one that should be scared.
However, I know that I behold something that is glimmering inside.
If not, then why are you are so attracted to me.
You are making me see how significant I really am.
So for that, I decided to pray and have faith that I will get these negative thoughts out of my head.
I really don't want to commit suicide or murder.
But sometimes I think that it is the only way out.
Which now I see is not true.
You are not worth it!
What about my family and friends?
What about them?
They love me more than I love myself.
I can't do that to them.
Their pain will last even after I am dead or in jail.
I love them more than you.
I need to tell someone that can help me.
There are people that specialize in this type of thing.
I don't want to be sad and depressed anymore because someone else is taking their insecurities out on me.
I am not going to destroy my life for you.
I am even going to spare your life.
Maybe when I am stronger, I will feel sorry for you, and I will even pray for you.
You did not break me.
You helped me to realize the power and potential that I behold

2

inside and out, which I plan to use in a positive way.
I am not as weak as I thought.
You are the weak one.
May God have mercy on your soul.

Signed
Truly,
I'm in Control.

What If?

What if I, he, she, them, or it.

What if this happened or what if that happened.

This would have happened, or this could have happened.

The What If game could be fun depending on what cards you have been dealt.

If you were dealt bad cards in the past, then the What If game could go on forever.

What if this, what if that.

The mystery of wondering how things could had been better or different, needs to stop.

You are torturing yourself.

Stop this game, do something positive to increase your morale.

Having faith, praying, seeking counseling, or even joining a support group can help you to heal.

Your cards have been damaged, whether you believe it or not.

What If is a never-ending game that can destroy you if you suffer from guilt, regret, and blame.

Forgiveness and sorry are the 2 cards in the game that you can pick voluntarily to make you a survivor.

Sometimes closure will be far away.

It comes with time and healing, so in the meanwhile you are reliving an infinite number of different moves repeatedly and it makes you addicted.

Don't get too comfortable doing that; it's counterproductive.

You must take control of the game and become active again.

Use your cards as a tool to help others get through this game too.

Turn that enormous hurt, pain, guilt, tears, and uncertain

emotion to an extremely passionate experience and wise conversation to educate others.

You have the power to inspire someone else to survive.

You can decide what cards you want to play next.

You can finally make the last move to live again.

What if that?

Help Us Protect the Children

Help us protect the children.
Stop participating in those dirty little secrets.
Don't pass on that shame and pain of this game.
Don't let your past, be their present and future.
Let them be free and innocent.
Let the children choose their preference.
Don't put your personal preference on them.
Don't spread this disease of sexual abuse.
It is too contagious.
Stop it and get help now.
I am so sorry that no one protected you!
I am so sorry that you had to keep this secret for so long!
You were the prey before you became the predator.
You didn't have the power back then, but you do now.
Give the children a fresh start because if you infect them, then
some of those kids will infect the smaller kids and others as
adults will continue to infect the children.
Break the cycle of this dirty little secret.
Don't pass on the shame, we need you to help us protect the
children.
It is the hidden disease that few are able and willing to talk
about because the innocent feels more guilty than the guilty
does.
However, there are so many people like you dealing with this
dirty little secret.
Stop whispering, sneaking, and passing it on.
Get help and stop, so that you can help us protect the children.
We can't stop this without you!

6

Her Final Performance

The curtains opened and closed, and I didn't even know the show was coming to an end.

While performing, she complained about her back and loss of appetite.

But her director said that she was ok.

She had been with that director for years, so she trusted her.

This seasoned director named Doc directed the show using her old fashion techniques with lack of technology, even in this day and time.

This did injustice to all of her actors and actresses because she lacks resources.

But Granny was comfortable with their relationship and that's all that mattered at the time.

Watching the show, I thought she was stressed.

I would say eat, drink, and get plenty of rest.

She finally went to another director, and he told her that she will be performing the role of her life impersonating the Big C in his play.

This was a role that she was not ready for, but she knew she had to do it.

The scenery was held in the pancreas which was a silent spot for the Big C.

She bypassed acts 1, 2, and 3 and jumped to act 4, that was the noticeable beginning and end.

At this point the new director told us to be very supportive and make this role comfortable for her.

For, she had months before she would make her final performance.

I said OMG, that's not a lot of time.

We had to get the tickets to be present in her final act.

Once we got to the play, we feared that at the end we would have to walk down the 5 steps of grief on our way out.

Denial would be step 1, anger would be step 2, and the other 3 would come right in order, one after the other.

You could tell her last performance was the hardest one, for she could barely walk at times.

She saw and spoke to people that had left the stage a long time ago.

She even added in childlike roles.

She was very diverse in her acting ability; I never knew that she was so talented.

Her new director said we would know when the play was coming to an end because she would take a few deep breaths and the lights will go out and the curtains will close.

When the curtains finally closed, we gave her a standing ovation because she played her most difficult role ever, successfully!

Was Alcohol Her Tool?

She used alcohol as her tool.
When she had it, she thought she could build anything.
When she was happy, she used it to brighten her day more.
She would be dancing, singing, and laughing with joy.
When she was angry, she used it to darken her day.
Use of profanity, rage, and sadness was the go-to.
When she didn't have it, all she did was think about it.
I thought alcohol was her tool but later realized that alcohol was using her as it's tool.
Alcohol used her to show that it was in total control.
It used her to show how it could get her to break up her family bonds.
It used her to show how it could break her body down.
Alcohol knew that once she used it, it would turn the situation around and use her.
Alcohol took her on a long journey until there was no more breath in her body.
So, was alcohol her tool? No, but it surely had her thinking that.

He Wanted All of Her

She had a relationship with a guy name Alcohol that no person could ever break up.

And I was so Jealous.

They were so tight that it was almost like they were one in the same.

However, if you knew her before him you could clearly see the difference now.

Sometimes they would fight, and she would distance herself from him.

But she always missed him greatly and went right back.

She thought he was so good to her.

He would tell her things that she wanted to hear.

He would take her to places that she wanted to go.

He could always relate to what she went through in the past.

He was very easy to contact for he was just on the next corner waiting to be picked up.

I was so jealous.

Sometimes, I would even try to get rid of him by kidnapping or drowning him in our sink.

However, she always found out and I would get fussed out.

He was so important to her, for she was willing to risk almost everything to be with him.

She never realized how mentally, physically, and emotionally abusive he was because of his soft voice and touches that she never even saw the real him coming.

Before he took all that he could take from her, he gave her a final kiss goodbye.

The funny thing is that all along he thought that he was the only one but happily he wasn't, when she was going through drama with him, she was calling God on the side.

Who's Bored?

Is the child that's reading under grade level bored?
Is the child that doesn't know his subject-verb agreement bored?
Is the child that can't do basic mathematics bored?
Is the child that doesn't do his homework bored?
Is the child that doesn't have any chores bored?
Why is the child bored when he has many things to do and learn?
This child really doesn't have time to be bored.
The world is passing this child by, and he doesn't even know it.
This child believes he must be entertained consistently by things that can only harm him.
Things that can only give him a false sense of hope and negative images.
Things that he uses by a push of a button technologically speaking.
This child says the word bored when he should use the statement unexposed intellectually.
However, the more the child is exposed to understandable knowledge, the more the child will want to learn.
Us as a community need to meet the child where he is and teach him something useful, meaningful, and new.
Our child really doesn't have the time to be bored.
Our child cannot afford to be bored.
Being bored is an illusion to cover up reality.

Wasted Energy

Why are you wasting your energy on fighting me?
All I want to do is educate you.
You are wasting your time laughing and joking.
Taking precious learning moments away from yourself and others.
It's not going to be funny once you take that placement test of life.
And end up on remedial level which will be your biggest fight.
You say that you only live once, that's why you need to enjoy life now.
And I reply what if you can live a long life, what will you have to show that sound.
Remember how much fun you had in class being disrespectful and being the class clown
or complaining saying this is stupid when you didn't have anything written down,
or saying I don't get it after you finished doing something other than paying attention?
Why do you disrespect the people that try to teach you, only to end up in suspension?

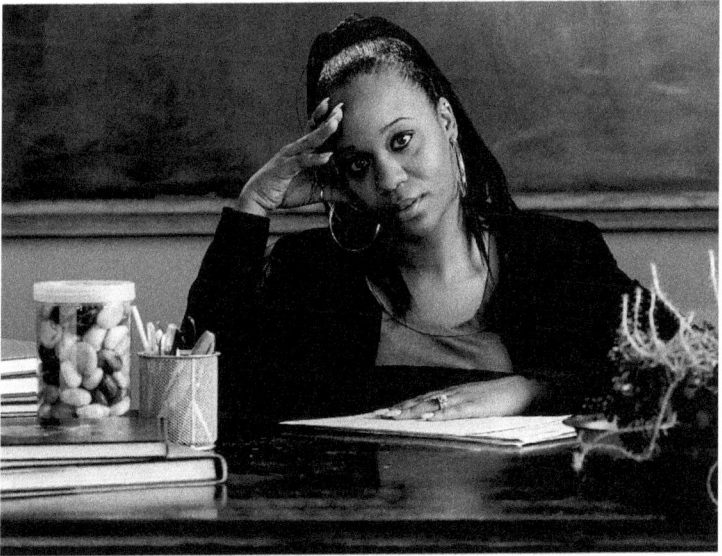

My Friend

I've noticed this year, that your visits are really becoming different. Every month is worse.
Not only are you running your mouth more, but you are really hurting my feelings.
It's becoming unbearable.
Some days when we hang out, I don't even want to leave the house.
I am scared that people may see my bruises that you left on me.
Your aggression is really affecting me.
Some days I feel so weak that I want to weep in the bed.
But, I just put on some extra armor and do my thing.
I miss the old you.
Recently, I've visited counselor to discuss new options on our relationship.
I just don't want to have that 10-month split from you like those times before the babies.
Each time was a surprise for me.
The counselor suggested another solution that might work for us.
I can't wait!
This type of relationship is too much for anyone!
Wow you are really a test for me, Alhamdulillah!

Call Me When It's Over

Wake Up!
Get Up!
And end this pity party now!
Don't get so comfortable with your situation.
This situation is slowly but surely destroying you.
No one really wants to come but this is the only event that you
are hosting these days.
It is sad that you don't realize how blessed you are.
Why focus on something that's not worth it?
You are having these parties too frequently.
You are wearing out all of your guests.
I for one, am tired of being a participant in your fun because
you are the only one benefiting these days, whether you believe
it or not.
I see now that I and others have been disabling you to strive by
attending these parties.
We have been letting you indulge in your misery.
Giving you all the attention.
Giving you advice that you never seem to take.
I am no longer attending your parties of misery.
Call me when the parties are over.
Goodbye!

You Don't Know Me

You don't know me because I only let you see what I wanted you to see.

You never saw the sadness and the anger within me.

You only saw the happiness and the smiles, under my mask.

You don't know me.

I am not the one to boohoo in public.

I just hold my feelings in until I am in a safe place.

You thought that you had me all figured out.

I wasn't like all of the rest; I didn't follow you in my heart.

I wasn't even scared or intimidated by you.

I just played the part of being the friendly person until that day when you tried me.

Being the professional that I am, I didn't result to the old me.

However, I did say to myself, "He really doesn't know who he is messing with?"

That was the day that I decided to show and tell everyone who I really was.

Not only am I fearless because I grew up in the inner-city projects of Baltimore, but I am Muslim and I only fear Allah (God), so I could never be a follower.

Man is not a threat to me.

You thought you knew me because you saw my external behavior.

Sadly, you know me now.

You never understood my faith because you thought your faith was superior.

That's the main thing that you should have been worried about.

A Man Doesn't Determine Your Worth

A man doesn't determine your worth.
You are responsible for your worth and your happiness.
If you let a man determine your worth, he can make you priceless one day and worthless the next.
You will be on an emotional roller coaster ride that never ends.
Only you can stop the ride by getting off.
You can do everything right, sacrifice everything, and still end up with nothing because you will never be enough in his eyes.
It's not you sis, it's him.
You will still have yourself and that priceless!
The great thing about this is you!
Even though it doesn't feel like it. You are everything!
You are worthy and you deserve the best!
Use that same energy and more that you put into him and give it to that person that deserves it the most, you.
It's time to show love to yourself limitlessly.

Be A Woman About It

Be a woman about it.
Express yourself emotionally.
Even if it's behind closed doors or in a place far away.
You don't have to let them see you sweat, cry, yell, or scream
but you must do it; release it to stay sane.
Free those emotions, so they don't build up.
If you don't you might end up in jail or in a mental institution
somewhere.
They don't understand anyway, they think that women are
crazy but that's not all the way true.
We are just a little emotionally unstable at times biologically
speaking.
We have our menstrual shows, our pregnancy parties, our
miscarriage movies, and our heated menopause and other
mysterious events.
We should be receiving all types of rewards for keeping it
together the way we do!
We might be emotionally confused inside sometimes but we
dress up and put on a smile and still run the show.
We are the great actors for we can play the happy, sad, and
angry role all in one scene.
Not only do we take care of everybody else, but we deal with
all their emotional baggage too while still carrying ourselves
extremely well.
We are beautiful and strong regardless of our physiological
changes.
They will never feel what we feel, so be yourself, accept
yourself, love yourself.

Don't imitate them.
You will go crazy trying to package all those feeling inside.
Express yourself emotionally even if it behind closed doors or in a place far away.
They don't have to see you sweat, cry, yell or scream but you must do it; release it to stay sane.

You Are Special

You are so special, that he wants to keep you all for himself.
He doesn't want you to shine because others might want you
too, so he keeps you in a box.
He tells you that you are not special, so that you don't shine too
bright.
Dimming your light, keeping the brightness from getting out.
You know deep down inside that you are still special because
other people have told you this before.
Hold onto those memories!
Try to remember who you were before you were a captive and
locked away.
Listen to those voices, remember those people, remember those
experiences, remember you!
You are still in there!
Get out of the box and shine bright like a diamond again.
Be the real you!
Be true to you!
Start now because it's time!

This Could Be My Time

This could be my time!
These ideas are keeping me up at night.
The possibilities are limitless.
The ideas are finally coming out.
I am so excited and energized.
Where do I start?
Should I finish what I started, or should I jump on this new idea?
All these years, I have been working for someone else's ideas.
Now that I am free, I feel encouraged to explore my ideas and dreams.
I am excited to implement these ideas.
This could be my time!

When Is It Your Time?

When is it your time?
Do you ask yourself this?
Is it today, tomorrow, when the kids are grown, or even when grandkids are grown too?
When is it your time?
After this is done or that is done?
Did you miss your time because you told yourself that?
It's too late, are you too old, or your time has passed?
If you are asking these questions, wake up for your time is now.
Get it together and live!
Live, Live, Live, Live your life!
Everyone that's living now has time now, so live before your time is really gone.

www.ingramcontent.com/pod-product-compliance
Lightning Source LLC
LaVergne TN
LVHW051818080426
835513LV00017B/2011